PYOTR IL'YICH TCHAIKOVSKY

ROMEO AND JULIET

Fantasy Overture
Third and final version (1880)

Ernst Eulenburg Ltd

London · Mainz · Madrid · New York · Paris · Prague · Tokyo · Toronto · Zürich

CONTENTS

PREFACE

In addition to purely symphonic works, Peter I. Tchaikovsky also wrote programmatic symphonic works. Here, Shakespeare evidently particularly inspired him in his own artistic creations, such as the Fantasy *The Tempest* and the Fantasy Overtures *Hamlet* as well as *Romeo and Juliet*. In Moscow during August 1869, the composer repeatedly met Mily A. Balakirev, whom he valued as an artist, though he found problematic his colleague's 'narrow views and his persistence in adhering to them'.[1] It was Balakirev, however, who aroused his interest in setting to music the Shakespeare *Romeo and Juliet* subject matter and immediately drafted for him a detailed programme with a formal structure and key plan. The result, Tchaikovsky's Fantasy Overture, ČW 39 (TchH 42), was premièred on 4/16 March 1870 (Julian/Gregorian calendar) with Nikolai G. Rubinstein as conductor in the 8th concert of the Russian Music Society in Moscow. Balakirev, though, criticised the overture and wrote in a letter of 9/21 May 1870, that '… much of it [= the overture] moves us to enthusiasm … But obvious flaws clearly show that the overture still has to be revised'.[2] So, the composer decided upon a radical reworking, which he undertook during a several-week spa cure in Bad Soden and stays in Interlaken and St. Petersburg. Eduard Fr. Napravnik christened the new version on 5/17 February 1872 in St. Petersburg at the 4th Russian Music Society concert. Yet, even the second version satisfied neither Tchaikovsky nor Balakirev ('I don't like the ending at all'):[3] the composer thereupon revised the overture again in the summer of 1880, albeit not so drastically. The original dedication to Mily Balakirev, omitted by the publisher when the revision was printed without involving Tchaikovsky, was reinstated in this third, final and nowadays established version of the Fantasy Overture. It was not premièred until 19 April/1 May 1886 in Tiflis [Tbilisi] by the Georgian branch of the Russian Music Society under the direction of the composer/conductor Mikhail M. Ippolitov-Ivanov. In 1884, incidentally, the publisher Belaieff had the composer sent anonymously 500 rubles for *Romeo and Juliet*.[4]

How specific Balakirev's ideas were for the programmatic interpretation and formal conception, can be seen in Nikolaj Kaškin's memoirs, where he reported in detail on Balakirev's programme draft, that 'he adapted to the sonata form: …first, a religiously-tempered introduction (Pater Lorenzo), then an Allegro in b minor (Balakirev had already mostly specified the keys), depicting the enmity between the Montagues and Capulets with their subsequent street confrontations, brawls, etc. Following was a transition to the love of Romeo and Juliet (second theme in D-flat major) and the conclusion of the exposition of the subject and the themes. The so-called development, that is, the confrontation of the themes in various forms and combinations, ended with the exposition's repetition, technically termed a recapitulation, with the first Allegro theme appearing in its original form and the love theme in D major. It all ends with the lovers' deaths.'[5]

The course does not precisely follow Shakespeare's model; perhaps one of the reasons why Tchaikovsky had trouble composing the work was: 'I haven't wanted to write you [= Balakirev] until now, because I have still not

---

[1] Tchaikovsky's letter of 11/23 August 1869, quoted from Elisabeth Bender, *Čajkovskijs Programmusik* (= *Čajkovskij-Studien 11*) (Mainz, 2009), 109. – The section on *Romeo and Juliet* (107–189) includes a comprehensive presentation of the genesis history and detailed analysis of the work.

[2] Quoted from Bender, 117.

[3] Balakirev's letter of 22 January/3 February 1871, quoted from Bender, 166.

[4] According to the *Tematiko-bibliografičeskij ykazatelj cočinenij P. I. Čajkovskogo* (= Thematic and bibliographical catalogue of P I. Tchaikovky's (P I. Čajkovkij's) works), eds. by Polina Vajdman, Ljudmila Korabel'nikova and Valentina Rubcova (Moscow, 2006), 355.

[5] Quoted from Bender, 109.

sketched anything for the overture. Imagine that I am completely empty and that not a single useful idea occurs to me. I am beginning to fear that my muse has flown far away.'[6] A few days later, though, Tchaikovsky reported work on a *Romeo and Juliet* overture to his brother Modest, who immediately replied: 'I am extremely astonished to learn that you are writing an overture *Romeo and Juliet*, first of all, because I recently read this work myself and composed an overture on it, and secondly, because without realising it, you've fulfilled one of my dearest wishes.'[7] Modest's programme differs from that by Balakirev, but the correspondence with his brother may have been the initial spark for Peter Tchaikovsky's own composition, the progress of which he reported a short time later to the one who had been the source of the idea. The work was finished on 15/27 November 1869.

From the outset, Tchaikovsky's Fantasy Overture suffered from the almost despotic influence of his colleague Balakirev, who had very specific ideas about how Tchaikovsky should implement the subject: He provided the sonata form as a model, linked characters and storylines of the Shakespearean drama with musical themes (with precise key information), so that the composer felt his inspiration to be constrained and hindered. Only during the course of revising did he break free and implement his concept, above all, in an individual formal structure: keys were changed, the introduction was rewritten in the second version, as were larger parts of the development and recapitulation. The composer devised a new coda. Modified in the final revised version were mainly the ending of the recapitulation and the coda, leaving in place the large-scale sonata form. The thematic fragmentation of the first version has yielded to a closed and more stringent resolution, even though certain themes can still be interpreted programmatically. After

a chorale-like, archaic sounding introduction, in which the winds dominate, characteristically evoking the spirit of Pater Lorenzo, the exposition – attained by an *accelerando* – begins with a striking theme, the "battle theme" – symbol of the warring Veronese aristocratic families. The lyrical "love theme" of the two protagonists then follows as the second theme. The development takes up both the introduction theme and the "battle theme", concluding after the recapitulation with a further developmental section and coda from the second version. The Fantasy Overture is indeed conceived as programme music, but warrants being considered as independent, absolute music even without the awareness of a dedicated programme. Tchaikovsky later contemplated writing an opera on the Shakespeare subject, though this was left as sketches and the fragment of a love duet (with material from the overture), which after the composer's death, Sergei I. Taneyev orchestrated and completed.

What has remained, however, is the powerful and poetic overture to *Romeo and Juliet* – a stirring and dramatic score, with rhythmically compact passages alternating with delicate, expressive moments, richly orchestrated with contrast and colour. The first version was not premièred under a lucky star: The conductor Nikolai G. Rubinstein, as director of the Moscow Conservatory, was having personal problems, dealing in court with a lawsuit. The verdict against him was overturned shortly before the concert, but it had become the focus of public interest – not the première of the work by Tchaikovsky, who was rather depressed by this response and lack of appreciation: 'My overture had no success here and remained completely unnoticed … And I was so eagerly awaiting a warm and empathetic word.'[8] Despite this disappointing start, the sombre work soon became one of Peter I. Tchaikovsky's most popular and often-played works. As early as 1873, the music critic (and Tchaikovsky friend) Hermann A. Laroche opined on the oc-

[6] Tchaikovsky's letter of 2/14 October 1869, quoted from Bender, 110.

[7] Modest I. Tchaikovsky's letter of 18/30 October 1869, quoted from Bender, 111.

[8] Letter to Ivan Klimenko from the night of 1 to 2/13 to 14 May 1870, quoted from Bender, 118.

casion of a concert in Moscow: 'There is currently much talk about this overture, especially in Petersburg, and I very much want to attest to its happy melodic inspirations, a noble harmony, a noteworthy mastery in the instrumentation and a charming poetry in many details.'[9]

This edition follows the first print of the score published by Bote & B. Bock, Berlin, 1881. Corrections and additions are identified.

Wolfgang Birtel
Translation: Margit L. McCorkle

---

[9] Quoted from Hermann Laroche, *Peter Tschaikowsky – Aufsätze und Erinnerungen.* Passages selected, translated and edited by Ernst Kuhn [= *musik konkret* 5] (Berlin, 1993), 75.

VORWORT

Peter I. Tschaikowsky schrieb neben rein symphonischen Werken auch solche mit programmatischem Bezug, wobei ihn Shakespeare offensichtlich besonders zu eigenem künstlerischen Schaffen animierte: mit der Fantasie *Der Sturm* und den Fantasie-Ouvertüren *Hamlet* sowie *Romeo und Julia*. Im August 1869 traf der Komponist in Moskau mehrfach Mili A. Balakirew, den er zwar als Künstler schätzte, mit dessen „Enge seiner Ansichten und [der] Hartnäckigkeit, mit der er daran [festhielt]"[1] er aber Probleme hatte. Der Komponistenkollege weckte in ihm das Interesse für eine Vertonung des Shakespeare-Stoffes *Romeo und Julia* und entwickelte sogleich einen detaillierten Programmentwurf mit formaler Struktur und Tonartenplan für ihn. Das Ergebnis, Tschaikowskys Fantasie-Ouvertüre, ČW 39 (TchH 42), wurde am 4./16. März 1870 (julianischer/gregorianischer Kalender) mit Nikolai G. Rubinstein als Dirigenten im 8. Konzert der Russischen Musikgesellschaft in Moskau uraufgeführt. Balakirew kritisierte die Ouvertüre allerdings und schrieb in einem Brief vom 9./21. Mai 1870, dass „… vieles von ihr [= der Ouvertüre] uns in Begeisterung versetzt … Aber offensichtliche Mängel zeigen deutlich, daß die Ouvertüre noch überarbeitet werden muß."[2] So entschloss sich der Komponist im Sommer 1870 zu einer tiefgreifenden Umarbeitung, die er während einer mehrwöchigen Kur in Bad Soden und Aufenthalten in Interlaken und St. Petersburg vornahm. Eduard Fr. Napravnik hob die neue Fassung am 5./17.2.1872 in St. Petersburg beim 4. Konzert der Gesellschaft aus der Taufe. Doch auch mit der zweiten Version waren sowohl Balakirew („… der Schluß gefällt mir

überhaupt nicht"[3]) wie auch der Komponist selbst nicht zufrieden: Im Sommer 1880 überarbeitete Tschaikowsky die Ouvertüre deshalb erneut, wenn auch nicht mehr so einschneidend. Die ursprüngliche Widmung an Mili Balakirew, die der Verleger beim Druck der Überarbeitung ohne Zutun des Komponisten weggelassen hatte, reaktivierte er in dieser dritten, nun endgültigen und heute etablierten Fassung der Fantasie-Ouvertüre. Sie wurde erst am 19.4./1.5.1886 in Tiflis von dem georgischen Zweig der Russischen Musikgesellschaft durch den Komponisten und Dirigenten Michail M. Ippolitow-Iwanow uraufgeführt. Der Verleger Belaieff ließ dem Komponisten im Übrigen 1884 anonym 500 Rubel für *Romeo und Julia* zukommen.[4]

Wie genau die Ideen zur programmatischen Ausdeutung und zur Formanlage des Werkes durch Balakirew waren, zeigt sich in den Erinnerungen Nikolaj Kaškins, der ausführlich über dessen Programmentwurf berichtete, dass „der sich an die Sonatenform anpaßte: … zunächst eine religiös gestimmte Einleitung (Pater Lorenzo), dann ein Allegro h-Moll (Balakirev hatte zumeist die Tonarten schon festgelegt), das die Feindschaft zwischen den Montagues und Capulets mit den mit ihr einhergehenden Straßenauseinandersetzungen, Handgemengen, etc. ausmalte. Danach folgte eine Überleitung zur Liebe von Romeo und Julia (zweites Thema Des-Dur) und der Abschluß der Exposition des Sujets und der Themen. Die sogenannte Durchführung, das heißt die Konfrontation der Themen in vielfältigen Formen und Kombinationen, endete mit der Wiederholung der Exposition, die man in der Fachsprache als Reprise be-

---

[1] Brief Tschaikowskys vom 11./23.8.1869, zit. nach Elisabeth Bender, Čajkovskijs Programmusik (= Čajkovskij-Studien 11), Mainz 2009, S. 109. – Der Abschnitt zu *Romeo und Julia* (S. 107–189) enthält eine umfassende Darstellung der Entstehungsgeschichte und eine eingehende Analyse des Werkes.
[2] Zit. nach Bender, S. 117.

[3] Brief Balakirews vom 22.1./3.2.1871, zit. nach Bender, S. 166.
[4] Lt. *Tematiko-bibliografičeskij ykazatelj cočinenij P. I. Čajkovskogo* (= Thematic and bibliographical catalogue of P I. Tchaikovky's (P I. Čajkovkij's) works), hg. v. Polina Vajdman, Ljudmila Korabel'nikova und Valentina Rubcova, Moskau 2006, S. 355.

zeichnet, wobei das erste Allegro-Thema in seiner ursprünglichen Gestalt und das Liebesthema in D-Dur auftreten. Alles endet dann mit dem Tod der Liebenden."[5]

Der Ablauf folgt nicht genau Shakespeares Vorlage; vielleicht einer der Gründe, warum Tschaikowsky Mühe hatte, das Werk zu komponieren: „Ich wollte Ihnen [= Balakirew] bis jetzt nicht schreiben, weil ich zur Ouvertüre noch nichts skizziert habe. Stellen Sie sich vor, daß ich vollkommen leer bin, und daß mir nicht eine einzige brauchbare Idee in den Kopf kommt. Ich fange an zu befürchten, daß meine Muse weit fortgeflogen ist."[6] Doch wenige Tage später berichtete Tschaikowsky seinem Bruder Modest, dass er an einer Ouvertüre *Romeo und Julia* arbeite, und der antwortete sofort: „Ich bin äußerst erstaunt zu erfahren, daß Du eine Ouvertüre *Romeo und Julia* schreibst, erstens, weil ich unlängst selbst dieses Werk gelesen habe und daraus eine Ouvertüre gedichtet habe, und zweitens, weil Du, ohne es zu ahnen, einen meiner sehnlichsten Wünsche erfüllt hast."[7] Modests Programm weicht von demjenigen Balakirews ab, doch mag die Korrespondenz mit dem Bruder sozusagen die Initialzündung für Peter Tschaikowskys eigene Komposition gewesen sein, von deren Fortschritt er kurze Zeit später dem Ideengeber berichtete. Am 15./27. November 1869 war das Werk beendet.

Tschaikowskys Fantasie-Ouvertüre litt von Anfang an unter dem geradezu despotischen Einwirken des Kollegen Balakirew, der sehr konkrete Vorstellungen davon hatte, wie Tschaikowsky das Sujet umsetzen solle: Er gab die Sonatenform als Modell vor, verknüpfte Charaktere und Handlungsstränge des Shakespeare-Dramas mit musikalischen Themen (mit genauen Tonarten-Angaben), so dass sich der Komponist eingezwängt und in seiner Inspiration behindert fühlte. Erst im Zuge der Überarbeitungen löste er sich von den Fesseln und setzte sein Konzept, vor allem eine individuelle formale Struktur um: Tonarten wurden geändert, die Einleitung wurde in der zweiten Version neu geschrieben, ebenso größere Teile der Durchführung und der Reprise. Der Komponist konzipierte eine neue Coda. In der letzten überarbeiteten Version wurden hauptsächlich der Schluss der Reprise und die Coda modifiziert. Geblieben ist die großformale Anlage der Sonatenform. Die thematische Zersplitterung der ersten Version ist aber einer geschlossenen und stringenteren Lösung gewichen, auch wenn nach wie vor bestimmte Themen durchaus programmatisch gedeutet werden können. Nach einer choralartigen, archaisch getönten Einleitung, in der die Bläser dominieren und die charaktermäßig den Geist von Pater Lorenzo beschwört, beginnt die – in einem Accelerando erreichte – Exposition mit einem markanten Thema, dem „Kampf-Thema" – Sinnbild der verfeindeten Veroneser Adelsfamilien. Im Seitensatz folgt dann das lyrische „Liebes-Thema" der beiden Protagonisten. Die Durchführung greift sowohl das Thema der Introduktion wie auch das „Kampfthema" auf, um nach der Reprise mit einem – ab der zweiten Fassung – weiteren Entwicklungsteil nebst Coda abzuschließen. Die Fantasie-Ouvertüre ist zwar als Programm-Musik konzipiert, hat aber auch ohne Kenntnis eines dezidierten Programmes seine Berechtigung als eigenständige, absolute Musik. Tschaikowsky trug sich später mit dem Gedanken, eine Oper über das Shakespeare-Sujet zu schreiben. Es blieb allerdings bei Skizzen und dem Fragment eines Liebes-Duetts (mit Material aus der Ouvertüre), das Sergei I. Tanejew nach des Komponisten Tod instrumentierte und ergänzte.

Geblieben ist aber die ebenso kraftvolle wie poetische Ouvertüre zu *Romeo und Julia* – eine aufrüttelnde und dramatische Partitur, mit rhythmisch-kompakten Passagen im Wechsel mit zarten, expressiven Momenten, kontrastreich und farbig instrumentiert. Die Uraufführung der ersten Fassung stand unter keinem guten Stern: Der Dirigent Nikolai G. Rubinstein hatte als Direktor des Moskauer Konservatoriums private Probleme, da er sich vor Gericht mit einer

[5] Zit. nach Bender, S. 109.
[6] Brief Tschaikowskys vom 2./14.10.1869, zit. nach Bender, S. 110.
[7] Brief Modest I. Tschaikowskys vom 18./30.10.1869, zit. nach Bender, S. 111.

IX

Beleidigungsklage auseinandersetzen musste. Das gegen ihn verkündete Urteil wurde zwar kurz vor dem Konzert kassiert, stand aber im Mittelpunkt des Publikumsinteresses – nicht die Uraufführung des Werkes von Tschaikowsky, der ob dieser Resonanz und der fehlenden Wertschätzung ziemlich deprimiert war: „Meine Ouvertüre hatte hier gar keinen Erfolg und blieb völlig unbemerkt … Und ich wartete so sehnlich auf ein warmes und mitfühlendes Wort."[8] Trotz dieses unerfreulichen Starts sollte das düstere Werk bald zu einem der beliebtesten und meist gespielten Werke von Peter I. Tschaikowsky werden. Schon 1873 urteilte der Musikkritiker (und Freund Tschaikowskys) Hermann A. Laroche anlässlich eines Konzertes in Moskau: „Von dieser Ouvertüre wird gegenwärtig viel geredet, namentlich in Petersburg, und ich will ihr gern glückliche melodische Eingebungen, eine edle Harmonik, eine bemerkenswerte Meisterschaft in der Instrumentierung und eine anmutige Poesie in vielen Details bescheinigen."[9]

Diese Ausgabe folgt dem Erstdruck der Partitur von Bote & G. Bock, Berlin 1881. Korrekturen und Ergänzungen sind kenntlich gemacht.

Wolfgang Birtel

---

[8] Brief an Ivan Klimenko in der Nacht vom 1. auf 2./vom 13. auf 14.5.1870, zit. nach Bender, S. 118.

[9] Zit. nach Hermann Laroche, *Peter Tschaikowsky – Aufsätze und Erinnerungen*. Ausgew., übers. und hg. von Ernst Kuhn (= *musik konkret 5*), Berlin 1993, S. 75.

ROMEO AND JULIET
Fantasy Overture

A Mr. Mily Balakirew

Pyotr Il'yich Tchaikovsky
(1840–1893)
ČW 39 (TchH 42)

EE 3793

6

*) Fg. 1: semibreve rest only in the score of the first print (=FP), in the part: D

14

*) Fl. 1: ♭ missing in FP

*) not in FP, editorial intervention

*) A# in FP

*) not in FP, editorial intervention

*) G♮ in FP